MESSAGE

OF THE

PRESIDENT OF THE UNITED STATES

TO THE

TWO HOUSES OF CONGRESS

AT

THE COMMENCEMENT OF THE FIRST SESSION OF THE FORTY-THIRD CONGRESS.

WASHINGTON:
GOVERNMENT PRINTING OFFICE.
1873.

MESSAGE.

To the Senate and House of Representatives:

The year that has passed since the submission of my last message to Congress has—especially during the latter part of it—been an eventful one to the country. In the midst of great national prosperity a financial crisis has occurred that has brought low fortunes of gigantic proportions; political partisanship has almost ceased to exist, especially in the agricultural regions; and finally, the capture upon the high seas of a vessel bearing our flag has for a time threatened the most serious consequences, and has agitated the public mind from one end of the country to the other. But this, happily, now is in the course of satisfactory adjustment, honorable to both nations concerned.

The relations of the United States, however, with most of the other powers continue to be friendly and cordial. With France, Germany, Russia, Italy, and the minor European powers; with Brazil and most of the South American republics, and with Japan, nothing has occurred during the year to demand special notice. The correspondence between the Department of State and various diplomatic representatives in or from those countries is transmitted herewith.

In executing the will of Congress, as expressed in its joint resolution of the 14th of February last, and in accordance with the provisions of the resolution, a number of "practical artisans," of "scientific men," and of "honorary commissioners" were authorized to attend the exposition at Vienna as commissioners on the part of the United States. It is believed that we have obtained the object which Congress had in view when it passed the joint resolution, "in order to enable the people of the United States to participate in the advantages of the international exhibition of the products of agriculture, manufactures, and the fine arts to be held at Vienna." I take pleasure in adding that the American exhibitors have received a gratifying number of diplomas and of medals.

During the exposition a conference was held at Vienna for the purpose of consultation on the systems prevailing in different countries for the protection of inventions. I authorized a representative from the Patent-Office to be present at Vienna at the time when this conference was to take place, in order to aid, as far as he might, in securing any possible additional protection to American inventors in Europe. The report of this agent will be laid before Congress.

It is my pleasant duty to announce to Congress that the Emperor of China, on attaining his majority, received the diplomatic representatives of the western powers in person. An account of these ceremonies, and of the interesting discussions which preceded them, will be found in the documents transmitted herewith. The accompanying papers show that some advance, although slight, has been made during the past year toward the suppression of the infamous Chinese cooly-trade. I recommend Congress to inquire whether additional legislation be not needed on this subject.

The money awarded to the United States by the tribunal of arbitration at Geneva was paid by Her Majesty's government a few days in advance of the time when it would have become payable according to the terms of the treaty. In compliance with the provisions of the act of March 3, 1873, it was at once paid into the Treasury, and used to redeem, so far as it might, the public debt of the United States; and the amount so redeemed was invested in a five per cent. registered bond of the United States for fifteen million five hundred thousand dollars, which is now held by the Secretary of State, subject to the future disposition of Congress.

I renew my recommendation, made at the opening of the last session of Congress, that a commission be created for the purpose of auditing and determining the amounts of the several "direct losses growing out of the destruction of vessels and their cargoes" by the Alabama, the Florida, or the Shenandoah, after leaving Melbourne, for which the sufferers have received no equivalent or compensation, and of ascertaining the names of the persons entitled to receive compensation for the same, making the computations upon the basis indicated by the tribunal of arbitration at Geneva; and that payment of such losses be authorized to an extent not to exceed the awards of the tribunal at Geneva.

By an act approved on the 14th day of February last, Congress made provision for completing, jointly with an officer or commissioner to be named by Her Britannic Majesty, the determination of so much of the boundary-line between the territory of the United States and the possessions of Great Britain as was left uncompleted by the commissioners appointed under the act of Congress of August 11, 1856. Under the provisions of this act the northwest water-boundary of the United States has been determined and marked in accordance with the award of the Emperor of Germany. A protocol and a copy of the map upon which the line was thus marked are contained in the papers submitted herewith.

I also transmit a copy of the report of the commissioner for marking the northern boundary between the United States and the British possessions west of the Lake of the Woods, of the operations of the commission during the past season. Surveys have been made to a point four hundred and ninety-seven miles west of the Lake of the Woods, leaving about three hundred and fifty miles to be surveyed, the field-work of which can be completed during the next season.

The mixed commission organized under the provisions of the treaty of Washington for settling and determining the claims of citizens of either power against the other arising out of the acts committed against their persons or property during the period between April 13, 1861, and April 9, 1865, made its final award on the 25th day of September last. It was awarded that the Government of the United States should pay to the government of Her Britannic Majesty, within twelve months from the date of the award, the sum of $1,929,819 in gold. The commission disallowed or dismissed all other claims of British subjects against the United States. The amount of the claims presented by the British government, but disallowed or dismissed, is understood to be about $93,000,000. It also disallowed all claims of citizens of the United States against Great Britain which were referred to it.

I recommend the early passage of an act appropriating the amount necessary to pay this award against the United States.

I have caused to be communicated to the government of the King of Italy the thanks of this Government for the eminent services rendered by Count Corti as the third commissioner on this commission. With dignity, learning, and impartiality he discharged duties requiring great labor and constant patience, to the satisfaction, I believe, of both governments. I recommend legislation to create a special court, to consist of three judges, who shall be empowered to hear and determine all claims of aliens upon the United States arising out of acts committed against their persons or property during the insurrection. The recent reference under the treaty of Washington was confined to claims of British subjects arising during the period named in the treaty; but it is understood that there are other British claims of a similar nature, arising after the 9th of April, 1865, and it is known that other claims of a like nature are advanced by citizens or subjects of other powers. It is desirable to have these claims also examined and disposed of.

Official information being received from the Dutch government of a state of war between the King of the Netherlands and the Sultan of Acheen, the officers of the United States who were near the seat of the war were instructed to observe an impartial neutrality. It is believed that they have done so.

The joint commission under the convention with Mexico of 1868 having again been legally prolonged, has resumed its business, which, it is hoped, may be brought to an early conclusion. The distinguished representative of Her Britannic Majesty at Washington has kindly consented, with the approval of his government, to assume the arduous and responsible duties of umpire in this commission, and to lend the weight of his character and name to such decisions as may not receive the acquiescence of both the arbitrators appointed by the respective governments.

The commissioners appointed pursuant to the authority of Congress to examine into the nature and extent of the forays by trespassers from that country upon the herds of Texas, have made a report, which will be submitted for your consideration.

The Venezuelan government has been apprised of the sense of Congress in regard to the awards of the joint commission under the convention of 25th April, 1866, as expressed in the act of the 25th of February last.

It is apprehended that that government does not realize the character of its obligations under that convention. As there is reason to believe, however, that its hesitancy in recognizing them springs in part at least from real difficulty in discharging them in connection with its obligations to other governments, the expediency of further forbearance on our part is believed to be worthy of your consideration.

The Ottoman government and that of Egypt have latterly shown a disposition to relieve foreign consuls of the judicial powers which heretofore they have exercised in the Turkish dominions, by organizing other tribunals. As Congress, however, has by law provided for the discharge of judicial functions by consuls of the United States in that quarter under the treaty of 1830, I have not felt at liberty formally to accept the proposed change without the assent of Congress, whose decision upon the subject, at as early a period as may be convenient, is earnestly requested.

I transmit herewith for the consideration and determination of Congress an application of the republic of Santo Domingo to this Government to exercise a protectorate over that republic.

Since the adjournment of Congress the following treaties with foreign powers have been proclaimed: A naturalization convention with Denmark; a convention with Mexico for renewing the claim commission; a convention of friendship, commerce, and extradition with the Orange Free State, and a naturalization convention with Ecuador.

I renew the recommendation made in my message of December, 1870, that Congress authorize the Postmaster-General to issue all commissions to officials appointed through his Department.

I invite the earnest attention of Congress to the existing laws of the United States respecting expatriation and the election of nationality by individuals. Many citizens of the United States reside permanently abroad with their families. Under the provisions of the act approved February 10, 1855, the children of such persons are to be deemed and taken to be citizens of the United States, but the rights of citizenship are not to descend to persons whose fathers never resided in the United States.

It thus happens that persons who have never resided within the United States have been enabled to put forward a pretension to the protection of the United States against the claim to military service of the government under whose protection they were born and have been reared. In some cases even naturalized citizens of the United States have returned to the land of their birth, with intent to remain there, and their children, the issue of a marriage contracted there after their return, and who have never been in the United States, have laid claim to our protection, when the lapse of many years had imposed upon them the duty of military service to the only government which had ever known them personally.

Until the year 1868 it was left embarrassed by conflicting opinions of courts and of jurists to determine how far the doctrine of perpetual allegiance derived from our former colonial relations with Great Britain was applicable to American citizens. Congress then wisely swept these doubts away by enacting that "any declaration, instruction, opinion, order, or decision of any officer of this Government which denies, restricts, impairs, or questions the right of expatriation, is inconsistent with the fundamental principles of this Government." But Congress did not indicate in that statute, nor has it since done so, what acts are deemed to work expatriation. For my own guidance in determining such questions, I required (under the provisions of the Constitution) the opinion in writing of the principal officer in each of the Executive Departments upon certain questions relating to this subject. The result satisfies me that further legislation has become necessary. I therefore commend the subject to the careful consideration of Congress, and I transmit herewith copies of the several opinions of the principal officers of the executive department, together with other correspondence and pertinent information on the same subject.

The United States, who led the way in the overthrow of the feudal doctrine of perpetual allegiance, are among the last to indicate how their own citizens may elect another nationality. The papers submitted herewith indicate what is necessary to place us on a par with other leading nations in liberality of legislation on this international question. We have already in our treaties assented to the principles which would need to be embodied in laws intended to accomplish such results. We have agreed that citizens of the United States may cease to be citizens, and may voluntarily render allegiance to other powers. We have agreed that residence in a foreign land, without intent to return, shall of itself work expatriation. We have agreed in some instances upon the length of time necessary for such continued residence to work a presumption of such intent. I invite Congress now to mark out and define when and how expatriation can be accomplished; to regulate by law the condition of American women marrying foreigners; to fix the status of children born in a foreign country of American parents residing more or less permanently abroad, and to make rules for determining such other kindred points as may seem best to Congress.

In compliance with the request of Congress I transmitted to the American minister at Madrid, with instructions to present it to the Spanish government, the joint resolution, approved on the 3d of March last, tendering to the people of Spain, in the name and on the behalf of the American people, the congratulations of Congress upon the efforts to consolidate in Spain the principles of universal liberty in a republican form of government.

The existence of this new republic was inaugurated by striking the fetters from the slaves in Porto Rico. This beneficent measure was followed by the release of several thousand persons illegally held as slaves in Cuba. Next, the captain-general of that colony was deprived of the power to set aside the orders of his superiors at Madrid, which had pertained to the office since 1825. The sequestered estates of American citizens, which had been the cause of long and fruitless correspondence, were ordered to be restored to their owners. All these liberal steps were taken in the face of a violent opposition directed by the reactionary slaveholders of Havana, who are vainly striving to stay the march of ideas which has terminated slavery in Christendom, Cuba only excepted. Unhappily, however, this baneful influence has thus far succeeded in defeating the efforts of all liberal-minded men in Spain to abolish slavery in Cuba, and in preventing the promised reform in that island. The struggle for political supremacy continues there.

The pro-slavery and aristocratic party in Cuba is gradually arraigning itself in more and more open hostility and defiance of the home government, while it still maintains a political connection with the republic in the peninsula; and although usurping and defying the authority of the home government, whenever such usurpation or defiance tends in the direction of oppression or of the maintenance of abuses, it is still a power in Madrid, and is recognized by the government. Thus an element more dangerous to continued colonial relations between Cuba and Spain than that which inspired the insurrection at Yara—an element opposed to granting any relief from misrule and abuse, with no aspirations after freedom, commanding no sympathies in generous breasts, aiming to rivet still stronger the shackles of slavery and oppression—has seized many of the emblems of power in Cuba, and, under professions of loyalty to the mother country, is exhausting the resources of the island, and is doing acts which are at variance with those principles of justice, of liberality, and of right, which give nobility of character to a republic. In the interests of humanity, of civilization, and of progress, it is to be hoped that this evil influence may be soon averted.

The steamer Virginius was on the 26th day of September, 1870, duly registered at the port of New York as a part of the commercial marine of the United States. On the 4th of October, 1870, having received the certificate of her register in the usual legal form, she sailed from the port of New York, and has not since been within the territorial jurisdiction of the United States. On the 31st day of October last, while sailing under the flag of the United States, on the high seas, she was forcibly seized by the Spanish gun-boat Tornado, and was carried into the port of Santiago de Cuba, where fifty-three of her passengers and crew were inhumanly, and, so far at least as relates to those who were citizens of the United States, without due process of law, put to death.

It is a well-established principle, asserted by the United States from the beginning of their national independence, recognized by Great Britain and other maritime powers, and stated by the Senate in a resolution passed unanimously on the 16th of June, 1858, that "American vessels on the high seas in time of peace, bearing the American flag, remain under the jurisdiction of the country to which they belong; and therefore any visitation, molestation, or detention of such vessel by force, or by the exhibition of force, on the part of a foreign power, is in derogation of the sovereignty of the United States."

In accordance with this principle the restoration of the Virginius, and the surrender of the survivors of her passengers and crew, and a due reparation to the flag, and the punishment of the authorities who had been guilty of the illegal acts of violence, were demanded. The Spanish government has recognized the justice of the demand, and has arranged for the immediate delivery of the vessel, and for the surrender of the survivors of the passengers and crew, and for a salute to the flag, and for proceedings looking to the punishment of those who may be proved to have been guilty of illegal acts of violence toward citizens of the United States, and also toward indemnifying those who may be shown to be entitled to indemnity. A copy of a protocol of a conference between the Secretary of State and the Spanish minister, in which the terms of this arrangement were agreed to, is transmitted herewith.

The correspondence on this subject with the legation of the United States in Madrid was conducted in cipher and by cable, and needs the verification of the actual text of the correspondence. It has seemed to me to be due to the importance of the case not to submit this correspondence until the accurate text can be received by mail. It is expected shortly, and will be submitted when received.

In taking leave of this subject for the present, I wish to renew the expression of my conviction, that the existence of African slavery in Cuba is a principal cause of the lamentable condition of the island. I do not doubt that Congress shares with me the hope that it will soon be made to disappear, and that peace and prosperity may follow its abolition.

The embargoing of American estates in Cuba; cruelty to American citizens detected in no act of hostility to the Spanish government; the murdering of prisoners taken with arms in their hands; and, finally, the capture upon the high seas of a vessel sailing under the United States flag and bearing a United States registry have culminated in an outburst of indignation that has seemed for a time to threaten war. Pending negotiations between the United States and the government of Spain on the subject of this capture, I have authorized the Secretary of the Navy to put our Navy on a war footing, to the extent, at least, of the entire annual appropriation for that branch of the service, trusting to Congress and the public opinion of the American people to justify my action.

CONSTITUTIONAL AMENDMENTS.

Assuming from the action of the last Congress, in appointing a "Committee on Privileges and Elections," to prepare and report to this Congress a constitutional amendment to provide a better method of electing the President and Vice-President of the United States, and also from the necessity of such an amendment, that there will be submitted to the State legislatures, for ratification, such an improvement in our Constitution, I suggest two others for your consideration:

First. To authorize the Executive to approve of so much of any measure passing the two Houses of Congress as his judgment may dictate, without approving the whole, the disapproved portion, or portions, to be subjected to the same rules as now, to wit, to be referred back to the house in which the measure, or measures, originated, and if passed by a two-thirds vote of the two houses, then to become a law without the approval of the President. I would add to this a provision that there should be no legislation by Congress during the last twenty-four hours of its sitting, except upon vetoes, in order to give the Executive an opportunity to examine and approve or disapprove bills understandingly.

Second. To provide, by amendment, that when an extra session of Congress is convened by Executive proclamation, legislation during the continuance of such extra session shall be confined to such subjects as the Executive may bring before it, from time to time, in writing.

The advantages to be gained by these two amendments are too obvious for me to comment upon them. One session in each year is provided for by the Constitution, in which there are no restrictions as to the subjects of legislation by Congress. If more are required, it is always in the power of Congress, during their term of office, to provide for sessions at any time. The first of these amendments would protect the public against the many abuses, and waste of public moneys, which creep into appropriation bills, and other important measures passing during the expiring hours of Congress, to which, otherwise, due consideration cannot be given.

TREASURY DEPARTMENT.

The receipts of the Government from all sources for the last fiscal year were $333,738,204, and expenditures on all accounts $290,345,245, thus showing an excess of receipts over expenditures of $43,392,959. But it is not probable that this favorable exhibit will be shown for the present fiscal year. Indeed, it is very doubtful whether, except with great economy on the part of Congress in making appropriations, and the same economy in administering the various departments of Government, the revenues will not fall short of meeting actual expenses, including interest on the public debt.

I commend to Congress such economy, and point out two sources where, it seems to me, it might commence, to wit, in the appropriations for public buildings in the many cities where work has not yet been commenced; in the appropriations for river and harbor improvement in those localities where the improvements are of but little benefit to general commerce, and for fortifications.

There is a still more fruitful source of expenditure, which I will point out later in this message. I refer to the easy method of manufacturing claims for losses incurred in suppressing the late rebellion.

I would not be understood here as opposing the erection of good, substantial, and even ornamental buildings by the Government wherever such buildings are needed. In fact, I approve of the Government owning its own buildings, in all sections of the country, and hope the day is not far distant when it will not only possess them, but will erect in the capital suitable residences for all persons who now receive commutation for quarters or rent at Government expense, and for the Cabinet, thus setting an example to the States which may induce them to erect buildings for their Senators. But I would have this work conducted at a time when the revenues of the country would abundantly justify it.

The revenues have materially fallen off for the first five months of the present fiscal year from what they were expected to produce, owing to the general panic now prevailing, which commenced about the middle of September last. The full effect of this disaster, if it should not prove a "blessing in disguise," is yet to be demonstrated. In either event it is your duty to heed the lesson, and to provide by wise and well-considered legislation, as far as it lies in your power, against its recurrence, and to take advantage of all benefits that may have accrued.

My own judgment is that, however much individuals may have suffered, one long step has been taken toward specie payments; that we can never have permanent prosperity until a specie basis is reached; and that a specie basis cannot be reached and maintained until our exports, exclusive of gold, pay for our imports, interest due abroad, and other specie obligations, or so nearly so as to leave an appreciable accumulation of the precious metals in the country from the products of our mines.

The development of the mines of precious metals during the past year and the prospective development of them for years to come, are gratifying in their results. Could but one-half of the gold extracted from the mines be retained at home our advance toward specie payments would be rapid.

To increase our exports, sufficient currency is required to keep all the industries of the country employed. Without this, national as well as individual bankruptcy must ensue. Undue inflation, on the other hand, while it might give temporary relief, would only lead to inflation of prices, the impossibility of competing in our own markets for the products of home skill and labor, and repeated renewals of present experiences. Elasticity to our circulating medium, therefore, and just enough of it to transact the legitimate business of the country, and to keep all industries employed, is what is most to be desired. The exact medium is specie, the recognized medium of exchange the world over. That obtained, we shall have a currency of an exact degree of elasticity. If there be too much of it for the legitimate purposes of trade and commerce, it will flow out of the country. If too little, the reverse will result. To hold what we have and to appreciate our currency to that standard, is the problem deserving of the most serious consideration of Congress.

The experience of the present panic has proven that the currency of the country, based as it is upon the credit of the country, is the best that has ever been devised. Usually in times of such trials, currency has become worthless, or so much depreciated in value as to inflate the values of all the necessaries of life as compared with the currency. Every one holding it has been anxious to dispose of it on any terms. Now we witness the reverse. Holders of currency hoard it as they did gold in former experiences of a like nature.

It is patent to the most casual observer that much more currency, or money, is required to transact the legitimate trade of the country during the fall and winter months, when the vast crops are being removed, than during the balance of the year. With our present system the amount in the country remains the same throughout the entire year, resulting in an accumulation of all the surplus capital of the country in a few centers when not employed in the moving of crops, tempted there by the offer of interest on call loans. Interest being paid, this surplus capital must earn this interest paid with a profit. Being subject to "call," it cannot be loaned, only in part at best, to the merchant or manufacturer for a fixed term. Hence, no matter how much currency there might be in the country, it would be absorbed, prices keeping pace with the volume, and panics, stringency, and disasters would ever be recurring with the autumn. Elasticity in our monetary system, therefore, is the object to be attained first, and next to that, as far as possible, a prevention of the use of other people's money in stock and other species of speculation. To prevent the latter it seems to me that one great step would be taken by prohibiting the national banks from paying interest on deposits, by requiring them to hold their reserves in their own vaults, and by forcing them into resumption, though it would only be in legal-tender notes. For this purpose I would suggest the establishment of clearing-houses for your consideration.

To secure the former many plans have been suggested, most, if not all, of which look to me more like inflation on the one hand, or compelling the Government, on the other, to pay interest, without corresponding benefits, upon the surplus funds of the country during the seasons when otherwise unemployed.

I submit for your consideration whether this difficulty might not be overcome by authorizing the Secretary of the Treasury to issue, at any time, to national banks of issue, any amount of their own notes below a fixed percentage of their issue, say forty per cent., upon the banks depositing with the Treasurer of the United States an amount of Government bonds equal to the amount of notes demanded, the banks to forfeit to the Government, say four per cent. of the interest accruing on the bonds so pledged during the time they remain with the Treasurer, as security for the increased circulation, the bonds so pledged to be redeemable by the banks at their pleasure, either in whole or in part, by returning their own bills for cancellation to an amount equal to the face of the bonds withdrawn. I would further suggest for your consideration the propriety of authorizing national banks to diminish their standing issue at pleasure, by returning for cancellation their own bills and withdrawing so many United States bonds as are pledged for the bills returned.

In view of the great actual contraction that has taken place in the currency, and the comparative contraction continuously going on, due to the increase of population, increase of manufactories, and all the industries, I do not believe there is too much of it now for the dullest period of the year. Indeed, if clearing-houses should be established, thus forcing redemption, it is a question for your consideration whether banking should not be made free, retaining all the safeguards now required to secure bill-holders. In any modification of the present laws regulating national banks, as a further step toward preparing for resumption of specie payments, I invite your attention to a consideration of the propriety of exacting from them the retention, as a part of their reserve, either the whole or a part of the gold interest accruing upon the bonds pledged as security for their issue. I have not reflected enough on the bearing this might have in producing a scarcity of coin with which to pay duties on imports to give it my positive recommendation. But your attention is invited to the subject.

During the last four years the currency has been contracted, directly, by the withdrawal of three per cent. certificates, compound-interest notes, and "seven-thirty" bonds outstanding on the 4th of March, 1869, all of which took the place of legal tenders in the bank reserves to the extent of sixty-three million dollars.

During the same period there has been a much larger comparative contraction of the currency. The population of the country has largely increased. More than twenty-five thousand miles of railroad have been built, requiring the active use of capital to operate them. Millions of acres of land have been opened to cultivation, requiring capital to move the products. Manufactories have multiplied beyond all precedent in the same period of time, requiring capital weekly for the payment of wages and for the purchase of material; and probably the largest of all comparative contraction arises from the organizing of free labor in the South. Now every laborer there receives his wages, and, for want of savings-banks, the greater part of such wages is carried in the pocket or hoarded until required for use.

These suggestions are thrown out for your consideration, without any recommendation that they shall be adopted literally, but hoping that the best method may be arrived at to secure such an elasticity of the currency as will keep employed all the industries of the country, and prevent such an inflation as will put off indefinitely the resumption of specie payments, an object so devoutly to be wished for by all, and by none more earnestly than the class of people most directly interested—those who "earn their bread by the sweat of their brow." The decisions of Congress on this subject will have the hearty support of the Executive.

In previous messages I have called attention to the decline in American ship-building, and recommended such legislation as would secure to us our proportion of the carrying-trade. Stimulated by high rates and abundance of freight, the progress for the last year in ship-building has been very satisfactory. There has been an increase of about three per cent. in the amount transported in American vessels over the amount of last year. With the reduced cost of material which has taken place, it may reasonably be hoped that this progress will be maintained, and even increased. However, as we pay about $80,000,000 per annum to foreign vessels for the transportation to a market of our surplus products, thus increasing the balance of trade against us to this amount, the subject is one worthy of your serious consideration.

"Cheap transportation" is a subject that has attracted the attention of both producers and consumers for the past few years, and has contributed to, if it has not been the direct cause of, the recent panic and stringency.

As Congress, at its last session, appointed a special committee to investigate this whole subject during the vacation, and report at this session, I have nothing to recommend until their report is read.

There is one work, however, of a national character, in which the greater portion of the East and the West, the North and the South, are equally interested, to which I will invite your attention.

The State of New York has a canal connecting Lake Erie with tide-water on the Hudson River. The State of Illinois has a similar work connecting Lake Michigan with navigable water on the Illinois River, thus making water-communication inland, between the East and the West and South. These great artificial water-courses are the property of the States through which they pass, and pay toll to those States. Would it not be wise statesmanship to pledge these States that if they will open these canals for the passage of large vessels the General Government will look after and keep in navigable condition the great public highways with which they connect, to wit, the overslaugh on the Hudson, the Saint Clair Flats, and the Illinois and Mississippi Rivers? This would be a national work; one of great value to the producers of the West and South in giving them cheap transportation for their produce to the sea-board and a market; and to the consumers in the East in giving them cheaper food, particularly of those articles of food which do not find a foreign market, and the prices of which, therefore, are not regulated by foreign demands. The advantages of such a work are too obvious for argument. I submit the subject to you, therefore, without further comment.

In attempting to regain our lost commerce and carrying-trade, I have heretofore called attention to the states south of us offering a field where much might be accomplished. To further this object I suggest that a small appropriation be made, accompanied with authority for the Secretary of the Navy to fit out a naval vessel to ascend the Amazon River to the mouth of the Madeira; thence to explore that river and its tributaries into Bolivia, and to report to Congress at its next session, or as soon as practicable, the accessibility of the country by water, its resources, and the population so reached. Such an exploration would cost but little; it can do no harm, and may result in establishing a trade of value to both nations.

In further connection with the Treasury Department I would recommend a revision and codification of the tariff laws, and the opening of more mints for coining money, with authority to coin for such nations as may apply.

WAR DEPARTMENT.

The attention of Congress is invited to the recommendations contained in the report of the Secretary of War herewith accompanying.

The apparent great cost of supporting the Army is fully explained by this report, and I hope will receive your attention.

While inviting your general attention to all the recommendations made by the Secretary of War, there are two which I would especially invite you to consider: First, the importance of preparing for war in time of peace by providing proper armament for our sea-coast defenses. Proper armament is of vastly more importance than fortifications. The latter can be supplied very speedily for temporary purposes when needed; the former cannot. The second is the necessity of re-opening promotion in the staff corps of the Army. Particularly is this necessity felt in the Medical, Pay, and Ordnance Departments.

At this time it is necessary to employ "contract surgeons" to supply the necessary medical attendance required by the Army.

With the present force of the Pay Department it is now difficult to make the payments to troops provided for by law. Long delays in payments are productive of desertions and other demoralization, and the law prohibits the payment of troops by other than regular Army paymasters.

There are now sixteen vacancies in the Ordnance Department, thus leaving that branch of the service without sufficient officers to conduct the business of the different arsenals on a large scale if ever required.

NAVY DEPARTMENT.

During the past year our Navy has been depleted by the sale of some vessels no longer fit for naval service, and by the condemnation of others not yet disposed of. This, however, has been more than compensated for by the repair of six of the old wooden ships, and by the building of eight new sloops of war, authorized by the last Congress. The building of these latter has occurred at a doubly fortunate time. They are about being completed at a time when they may possibly be much needed, and the work upon them has not only given direct employment to thousands of men, but has no doubt been the means of keeping open establishments for other work at a time of great financial distress.

Since the commencement of the last month, however, the distressing occurrences which have taken place in the waters of the Caribbean Sea, almost on our very sea-board, while they illustrate most forcibly the necessity always existing that a nation situated like ours should maintain in a state of possible efficiency a navy adequate to its responsibilities, has at the same time demanded that all the effective force we really have shall be put in immediate readiness for warlike service. This has been and is being done promptly and effectively, and I am assured that all the available ships and every authorized man of the American Navy will be ready for whatever action is required for the safety of our citizens or the maintenance of our honor. This, of course, will require the expenditure in a short time of some of the appropriations which were calculated to extend through the fiscal year, but Congress will, I doubt not, understand and appreciate the emergency, and will provide adequately, not only for the present preparation, but for the future maintenance of our naval force. The Secretary of the Navy has, during the past year, been quietly putting some of our most effective monitors in condition for service, and thus the exigency finds us in a much better condition for work than we could possibly have been without his action.

POST-OFFICE DEPARTMENT.

A complete exhibit is presented, in the accompanying report of the Postmaster-General, of the operations of the Post-Office Department during the year. The ordinary postal revenues for the fiscal year ended June 30, 1873, amounted to $22,996,741.57, and the expenditures of all kinds to $29,084,945.67. The increase of revenues over 1872 was $1,081,315.20, and the increase of expenditures $2,426,753.36.

Independent of the payments made from special appropriations for mail-steamship lines, the amount drawn from the general Treasury to meet deficiencies was $5,265,475. The constant and rapid extension of our postal service, particularly upon railways, and the improved facilities for the collection, transmission, distribution, and delivery of the mails, which are constantly being provided, account for the increased expenditures of this popular branch of the public service.

The total number of post-offices in operation, on June 30, 1873, was 33,244, a net increase of 1,381 over the number reported the preceding year. The number of presidential offices was 1,363, an increase of 163 during the year. The total length of railroad mail-routes at the close of the year was 63,457 miles, an increase of 5,546 miles over the year 1872. Fifty-nine railway post-office lines were in operation June 30, 1873, extending over 14,866 miles of railroad-routes, and performing an aggregate service of 34,925 miles daily.

The number of letters exchanged with foreign countries was 27,459,185, an increase of 3,096,685 over the previous year, and the postage thereon amounted to $2,021,310.86. The total weight of correspondence exchanged in the mails with European countries exceeded 912 tons, an increase of 92 tons over the previous year. The total cost of the United States ocean-steamship service, including $725,000 paid from special appropriations to subsidized lines of mail-steamers, was $1,047,271.35.

New or additional postal conventions have been concluded with Sweden, Norway, Belgium, Germany, Canada, Newfoundland, and Japan, reducing postage rates on correspondence exchanged with those countries; and further efforts have been made to conclude a satisfactory postal convention with France, but without success.

I invite the favorable consideration of Congress to the suggestions and recommendations of the Postmaster-General for an extension of the free-delivery system in all cities having a population of not less than ten thousand; for the prepayment of postage on newspapers and other printed matter of the second class; for a uniform postage and limit of weight on miscellaneous matter; for adjusting the compensation of all postmasters not appointed by the President, by the old method of commissions on the actual receipts of the office, instead of the present mode of fixing the salary in advance upon special returns; and especially do I urge favorable action by Congress on the important recommendations of the Postmaster-General for the establishment of United States postal savings depositories.

Your attention is also again called to a consideration of the question of postal telegraphs, and the arguments adduced in support thereof, in the hope that you may take such action in connection therewith as in your judgment will most contribute to the best interests of the country.

DEPARTMENT OF JUSTICE.

Affairs in Utah require your early and special attention. The Supreme Court of the United States, in the case of Clinton *vs.* Englebrecht, decided that the United States marshal of that Territory could not lawfully summon jurors for the district courts; and those courts hold that the territorial marshal cannot lawfully perform that duty, because he is elected by the legislative assembly and not appointed as provided for in the act organizing the Territory. All proceedings at law are practically abolished by these decisions, and there have been but few or no jury trials in the district courts of that Territory since the last session of Congress. Property is left without protection by the courts, and crimes go unpunished. To prevent anarchy there, it is absolutely necessary that Congress provide the courts with some mode of obtaining jurors, and I recommend legislation to that end; and also that the probate courts of the Territory, now assuming to issue writs of injunction and *habeas corpus*, and to try criminal cases and questions as to land-titles, be denied all jurisdiction not possessed ordinarily by courts of that description.

I have become impressed with the belief that the act approved March 2, 1867, entitled "An act to establish a uniform system of bankruptcy throughout the United States," is productive of more evil than good at this time. Many considerations might be urged for its total repeal, but, if this is not considered advisable, I think it will not be seriously questioned that those portions of said act providing for what is called involuntary bankruptcy operate to increase the financial embarrassments of the country. Careful and prudent men very often become involved in debt in the transaction of their business, and though they may possess ample property, if it could be made available for that purpose, to meet all their liabilities, yet, on account of the extraordinary scarcity of money, they may be unable to meet all their pecuniary obligations as they become due, in consequence of which they are liable to be prostrated in their business by proceedings in bankruptcy at the instance of unrelenting creditors. People are now so easily alarmed as to monetary matters that the mere filing of a petition in bankruptcy by an unfriendly creditor will necessarily embarrass, and oftentimes accomplish the financial ruin of a responsible business man. Those who otherwise might make lawful and just arrangements to relieve themselves from difficulties produced by the present stringency in money, are prevented by their constant exposure to attack and disappointment by proceedings against them in bankruptcy, and, beside, the law is made use of in many cases by obdurate creditors to frighten or force debtors into a compliance with their wishes and into acts of injustice to other creditors and to themselves. I recommend that so much of said act as provides for involuntary bankruptcy on account of the suspension of payment be repealed.

Your careful attention is invited to the subject of claims against the Government, and to the facilities afforded by existing laws for their prosecution. Each of the Departments of State, Treasury, and War have demands for many millions of dollars upon their files, and they are rapidly accumulating. To these may be added those now pending before Congress, the Court of Claims, and the southern claims commission, making in the aggregate an immense sum. Most of these grow out of the rebellion, and are intended to indemnify persons on both sides for their losses during the war; and not a few of them are fabricated and supported by false testimony. Projects are on foot, it is believed, to induce Congress to provide for new classes of claims, and to revive old ones through the repeal or modification of the statute of limitations, by which they are now barred. I presume these schemes, if proposed, will be received with little favor by Congress, and I recommend that persons having claims against the United States cognizable by any tribunal or department thereof, be required to present them at an early day, and that legislation be directed as far as practicable to the defeat of unfounded and unjust demands upon the Government; and I would suggest, as a means of preventing fraud, that witnesses be called upon to appear in person to testify before those tribunals having said claims before them for adjudication. Probably the largest saving to the national Treasury can be secured by timely legislation on these subjects, of any of the economic measures that will be proposed.

You will be advised of the operations of the Department of Justice by the report of the Attorney-General, and I invite your attention to the amendments of existing laws suggested by him, with the view of reducing the expenses of that Department.

DEPARTMENT OF THE INTERIOR.

The policy inaugurated toward the Indians at the beginning of the last administration has been steadily pursued, and, I believe, with beneficial results. It will be continued with only such modifications as time and experience may demonstrate as necessary.

With the encroachment of civilization upon the Indian reservations and hunting-grounds, disturbances have taken place between the Indians and whites during the past year, and probably will continue to do so until each race appreciates that the other has rights which must be respected.

The policy has been to collect the Indians, as rapidly as possible, on reservations—and as far as practicable within what is known as the Indian Territory—and to teach them the arts of civilization and self-support. Where found off their reservations, and endangering the peace and safety of the whites, they have been punished, and will continue to be for like offenses.

The Indian Territory south of Kansas and west of Arkansas is sufficient in area and agricultural resources to support all the Indians east of the Rocky Mountains. In time, no doubt, all of them, except a few who may select to make their homes among white people, will be collected there. As a preparatory step for this consummation, I am now satisfied that a territorial form of government should be given them, which will secure the treaty rights of the original settlers, and protect their homesteads from alienation for a period of twenty years.

The operations of the Patent-Office are growing to such a magnitude, and the accumulation of material is becoming so great, that the necessity for more room is becoming more obvious day by day. I respectfully invite your attention to the reports of the Secretary of the Interior and Commissioner of Patents on this subject.

The business of the General Land-Office exhibits a material increase in all its branches during the last fiscal year. During that time there were disposed of, out of the public lands, 13,030,606 acres, being an amount greater by 1,165,631 acres than was disposed of during the preceding year. Of the amount disposed of 1,626,266 acres were sold for cash; 214,940 acres were located with military land-warrants; 3,793,612 acres were taken for homesteads; 653,446 acres were located with agricultural-college scrip; 6,083,536 acres were certified by railroads; 76,576 acres were granted to wagon-roads; 238,548 acres were approved to States as swamp-lands; 138,681 acres were certified for agricultural colleges, common schools, universities, and seminaries; 190,775 acres were approved to States for internal improvements; and 14,222 acres were located with Indian scrip. The cash receipts during the same time were $3,408,515.50, being $190,415.50 in excess of the receipts of the previous year. During the year 30,488,132 acres of public land were surveyed, an increase over the amount surveyed the previous year of 1,037,193 acres, and, added to the area previously surveyed, aggregates 616,554,895 acres which have been surveyed, leaving 1,218,443,505 acres of the public land still unsurveyed.

The increased and steadily increasing facilities for reaching our unoccupied public domain, and for the transportation of surplus products, enlarges the available field for desirable homestead locations, thus stimulating settlement and extending year by year in a gradually increasing ratio the area of occupation and cultivation.

The expressed desire of the representatives of a large colony of citizens of Russia to emigrate to this country, as is understood, with the consent of their government, if certain concessions can be made to enable them to settle in a compact colony, is of great interest, as going to show the light in which our institutions are regarded by an industrious, intelligent, and wealthy people, desirous of enjoying civil and religious liberty; and the acquisition of so large an immigration of citizens of a superior class would, without doubt, be of substantial benefit to the country. I invite attention to the suggestion of the Secretary of the Interior in this behalf.

There was paid during the last fiscal year for pensions, including the expense of disbursement, $29,185,289.62, being an amount less by $984,050.98 than was expended for the same purpose the preceding year. Although this statement of expenditures would indicate a material reduction in amount compared with the preceding year, it is believed that the changes in the pension-laws at the last session of Congress will absorb that amount the current year. At the close of the last fiscal year there were on the pension-rolls 99,804 invalid military pensioners and 112,088 widows, orphans, and dependent relatives of deceased soldiers, making a total of that class of 211,892; 18,266 survivors of the war of 1812, and 5,053 widows of soldiers of that war pensioned under the act of Congress of February 14, 1871, making a total of that class of 23,319; 1,430 invalid Navy pensioners, and 1,770 widows, orphans, and dependent relatives of deceased officers, sailors, and marines of the Navy, making a total of Navy pensioners of 3,200, and a grand total of pensioners of all classes of 238,411, showing a net increase during the last fiscal year of 6,182. During the last year the names of 16,405 pensioners were added to the rolls, and 10,223 names were dropped therefrom for various causes.

The system adopted for the detection of frauds against the Government in the matter of pensions has been productive of satisfactory results, but legislation is needed to provide, if possible, against the perpetration of such frauds in future.

The evidently increasing interest in the cause of education is a most encouraging feature in the general progress and prosperity of the country, and the Bureau of Education is earnest in its efforts to give proper direction to the new appliances and increased facilities which are being offered to aid the educators of the country in their great work.

The ninth census has been completed, the report thereof published and distributed, and the working force of the bureau disbanded. The Secretary of the Interior renews his recommendation for a census to be taken in 1875, to which subject the attention of Congress is invited The original suggestion in that behalf has met with the general approval of the country, and even if it be not deemed advisable at present to provide for a regular quinquennial census, a census taken in 1875, the report of which could be completed and published before the one hundredth anniversary of our national independence, would be especially interesting and valuable, as showing the progress of the country during the first century of our national existence. It is believed, however, that a regular census every five years would be of substantial benefit to the country, inasmuch as our growth hitherto has been so rapid that the results of the decennial census are necessarily unreliable as a basis of estimates for the latter years of a decennial period.

DISTRICT OF COLUMBIA.

Under the very efficient management of the governor and the board of public works of this District, the city of Washington is rapidly assuming the appearance of a capital of which the nation may well be proud. From being a most unsightly place three years ago, disagreeable to pass through in summer in consequence of the dust arising from unpaved streets, and almost impassable in the winter from the mud, it is now one of the most sightly cities in the country, and can boast of being the best paved.

The work has been done systematically, the plans, grades, location of sewers, water and gas mains being determined upon before the work was commenced, thus securing permanency when completed. I question whether so much has ever been accomplished before in any American city for the same expenditures. The Government having large reservations in the city, and the nation at large having an interest in their capital, I recommend a liberal policy toward the District of Columbia, and that the Government should bear its just share of the expense of these improvements. Every citizen visiting the capital feels a pride in its growing beauty, and that he too is part owner of the investments made here.

I would suggest to Congress the propriety of promoting the establishment in this District of an institution of learning, or university of the highest class, by the donation of lands. There is no place better suited for such an institution than the national capital. There is no other place in which every citizen is so directly interested.

CIVIL-SERVICE REFORM.

In three successive messages to Congress I have called attention to the subject of "civil-service reform."

Action has been taken so far as to authorize the appointment of a board to devise rules governing methods of making appointments and promotions, but there never has been any action making these rules, or any rules, binding, or even entitled to observance where persons desire the appointment of a friend, or the removal of an official who may be disagreeable to them.

To have any rules effective they must have the acquiescence of Congress as well as of the Executive. I commend, therefere, the subject to your attention, and suggest that a special committee of Congress might confer with the civil-service board during the present session for the purpose of devising such rules as can be maintained, and which will secure the services of honest and capable officials, and which will also protect them in a degree of independence while in office.

Proper rules will protect Congress, as well as the Executive, from much needless persecution, and will prove of great value to the public at large.

I would recommend for your favorable consideration the passage of an enabling act for the admittance of Colorado as a State in the Union. It possesses all the elements of a prosperous State, agricultural and mineral, and, I believe, has a population now to justify such admission. In connection with this I would also recommend the encouragement of a canal for purposes of irrigation from the eastern slope of the Rocky Mountains to the Missouri River. As a rule, I am opposed to further donations of public lands for internal improvements, owned and controlled by private corporations, but in this instance I would make an exception. Between the Missouri River and the Rocky Mountains there is an arid belt of public land from three hundred to five hundred miles in width, perfectly valueless for the occupation of man, for the want of sufficient rain to secure the growth of any product. An irrigating-canal would make productive a belt, as wide as the supply of water could be made to spread over, across this entire country, and would secure a cordon of settlements, connecting the present population of the mountain and mining regions with that of the older States. All the land reclaimed would be clear gain. If alternate sections are retained by the Government, I would suggest that the retained sections be thrown open to entry under the homestead laws, or sold to actual settlers for a very low price.

I renew my previous recommendation to Congress for general amnesty. The number engaged in the late rebellion yet laboring under disabilities is very small, but enough to keep up a constant irritation. No possible danger can accrue to the Government by restoring them to eligibility to hold office.

I suggest for your consideration the enactment of a law to better secure the civil rights which freedom should secure, but has not effectually secured, to the enfranchised slave.

U. S. GRANT.

EXECUTIVE MANSION, *December* 1, 1873.

Protocol of the conference held at the Department of State, at Washington, on the 29th of November, 1873, between Hamilton Fish, Secretary of State, and Rear-Admiral Don José Polo de Bernabé, envoy extraordinary and minister plenipotentiary of Spain.

The undersigned having met for the purpose of entering into a definitive agreement respecting the case of the steamer Virginius, which, while under the flag of the United States, was, on the 31st day of October last, captured on the high seas by the Spanish man-of-war Tornado, have reached the following conclusions:

Spain, on her part, stipulates to restore forthwith the vessel referred to, and the survivors of her passengers and crew, and on the 25th day of December next to salute the flag of the United States. If, however, before that date Spain should prove to the satisfaction of the Government of the United States that the Virginius was not entitled to carry the flag of the United States, and was carrying it, at the time of her capture, without right and improperly, the salute will be spontaneously dispensed with, as in such case not being necessarily requirable; but the United States will expect, in such case, a disclaimer of the intent of indignity to its flag in the act which was committed.

Furthermore, if on or before the 25th of December, 1873, it shall be made to appear to the satisfaction of the United States that the Virginius did not rightfully carry the American flag and was not entitled to American papers, the United States will institute inquiry, and adopt legal proceedings against the vessel, if it be found that she has violated any law of the United States, and against any of the persons who may appear to have been guilty of illegal acts in connection therewith; it being understood that Spain will proceed, according to the second proposition made to General Sickles, and communicated in his telegram read to Admiral Polo on the 27th instant, to investigate the conduct of those of her authorities who have infringed Spanish laws or treaty obligations, and will arraign them before competent courts and inflict punishment on those who may have offended.

Other reciprocal reclamations to be the subject of consideration and arrangement between the two governments; and in case of no agreement, to be the subject of arbitration if the constitutional assent of the Senate of the United States be given thereto.

It is further stipulated that the time, manner, and place for the surrender of the Virginius, and the survivors of those who were on board of her at the time of her capture, and also the time, manner, and place for the salute to the flag of the United States, if there should be occasion for such salute, shall be subject to arrangement between the undersigned, within the next two days.

HAMILTON FISH.
JOSÉ POLO DE BERNABÉ.

No. 182½.*

PROTOCOL.

Whereas it was provided by the first article of the treaty between the United States of America and Great Britain, signed at Washington on the 15th of June, 1846, as follows:

"ARTICLE I.

"From the point on the 49th parallel of north latitude where the boundary laid down in existing treaties and conventions between the United States and Great Britain terminates, the line of boundary between the territories of the United States and those of Her Britannic Majesty shall be continued westward along the said 49th parallel of north latitude to the middle of the channel which separates the continent from Vancouver's Island; and thence southerly, through the middle of the said channel and of Fuca Straits, to the Pacific Ocean: *Provided, however*, That the navigation of the whole of the said channel and straits south of the 49th parallel of north latitude remain free and open to both parties."

And whereas it was provided by the XXXIVth Article of the treaty between the United States of America and Great Britain, signed at Washington on the 8th of May, 1871, as follows:

"ARTICLE XXXIV.

"Whereas it was stipulated by Article I of the treaty concluded at Washington on the 15th of June, 1846, between the United States and Her Britannic Majesty, that the line of boundary between the territories of the United States and those of Her Britannic Majesty, from the point on the 49th parallel of north latitude up to which it had already been ascertained, should be continued westward along the said parallel of north latitude to the middle of the channel which separates the continent from Vancouver's Island, and thence southerly, through the middle of the said channel and of Fuca Straits, to the Pacific Ocean; and whereas the commissioners appointed by the two high contracting parties to determine that portion of the boundary which runs southerly through the middle of the channel aforesaid were unable to agree upon the same; and whereas the government of Her Britannic Majesty claims that such boundary-line should, under the terms of the treaty above recited, be run through the Rosario Straits, and the Government of the United States claims that it should be run through the Canal de Haro, it is agreed that the respective claims of the Government of the United States and of the government of Her Britannic Majesty shall be submitted to the arbitration and award of His Majesty the Emperor of Germany, who, having regard to the above-mentioned article of the said treaty, shall decide thereupon, finally and without appeal, which of those claims is most in accordance with the true interpretation of the treaty of June 15, 1846."

And whereas His Majesty the Emperor of Germany has, by his award

* This should have been inserted on page 418. It was omitted by mistake in the manuscript transmitted to the printer.

dated the 21st of October, 1872, decided that "Mit der richtigen Auslegung des zwischen den Regierungen Ihrer Britischen Majestät und der Vereinigten Staaten Von Amerika geschlossenen Vertrages de dato Washington den 15 Juni, 1846, steht der Anspruch der Regierung der Vereinigten Staaten am meisten im Einklange, dass die Grenzlinie zwischen den Gebieten Ihrer Britischen Majestät und den Vereinigten Staaten durch den Haro-Kanal gezogen werde."

The undersigned, Hamilton Fish, Secretary of State of the United States, and the Right Honourable Sir Edward Thornton, one of Her Majesty's Most Honourable Privy Council, Knight Commander of the Most Honourable Order of the Bath, Her Britannic Majesty's Envoy Extraordinary and Minister Plenipotentiary to the United States of America, and Rear-Admiral James Charles Prevost, Commissioner of Her Britannic Majesty in respect of the boundary aforesaid, duly authorized by their respective governments to trace out and mark, on charts prepared for that purpose, the line of boundary in conformity with the award of His Majesty the Emperor of Germany, and to complete the determination of so much of the boundary-line between the territory of the United States and the possessions of Great Britain as was left uncompleted by the commissioners heretofore appointed to carry into effect the first article of the treaty of 15th June, 1846, have met together at Washington, and have traced out and marked the said boundary-line on four charts, severally entitled, "North America, West Coast, Strait of Juan de Fuca, and the channels between the continent and Vancouver Id, showing the boundary-line between British and American possessions, from the admiralty surveys by Captains H. Kellett, R. N., 1847, and G. H. Richards, R. N., 1858–1862;" and having on examination agreed that the lines so traced out and marked on the respective charts are identical, they have severally signed the said charts on behalf of their respective Governments, two copies thereof to be retained by the Government of the United States, and two copies thereof to be retained by the Government of Her Britannic Majesty, to serve with the "definition of the boundary-line," attached hereto, showing the general bearings of the line of boundary as laid down on the charts, as a perpetual record of agreement between the two governments in the matter of the line of boundary between their respective dominions under the first article of the treaty concluded at Washington on the 15th of June, 1846.

In witness whereof the undersigned have signed this protocol, and have hereunto affixed their seals.

Done in duplicate at Washington, this tenth day of March, in the year 1873.

HAMILTON FISH. [SEAL.]
EDWD. THORNTON. [SEAL.]
JAMES C. PREVOST. [SEAL.]

DEFINITION OF THE BOUNDARY-LINE.

The chart upon which the boundary-line between the British and the United States possessions is laid down is entitled "North America, West Coast, Strait of Juan de Fuca, and the channels between the continent and Vancouver Id, showing the boundary-line between British and American possessions, from the admiralty surveys by Captains H. Kellett, R. N., 1847, and G. H. Richards, R. N., 1858–1862."

The boundary-line thus laid down on the chart is a black line shaded red on the side of the British possessions, and blue on the side of the possessions of the United States.

The boundary-line thus defined commences at the point on the 49th parallel of north latitude on the west side of Point Roberts, which is marked by a stone monument, and the line is continued along the said parallel to the middle of the channel which separates the continent from Vancouver Island, that is to say, to a point in longitude 123° 19′ 15″ W., as shown in the said chart. It then proceeds in a direction about S. 50° E. (true) for about fifteen geographical miles, when it curves to the southward, passing equidistant between the west point of Patos Island and the east point of Saturna Island, until the point midway on a line drawn between Turnpoint, on Stewart Island, and Fairfax Point, on Moresby Island, bears S. 68° W., (true,) distant ten miles; then on a course south 68° W., (true,) ten miles to the said point midway between Turnpoint, on Stewart Island, and Fairfax Point, on Moresby Island; thence on a course about south 12° 30′ east (true) for about eight and three-quarter miles to a point due east, one mile from the northernmost Kelp Reef, which reef on the said chart is laid down as in latitude 48° 33′ north, and in longitude 123° 15′ west; then its direction continues about S. 20° 15′ east, (true,) six and one-eighth miles to a point midway between Sea Bird Point, on Discovery Island, and Pile Point, on San Juan Island; thence in a straight line S. 45° E., (true,) until it touches the north end of the middle bank in between 13 and 18 fathoms of water; from this point the line takes a general S. 28° 30′ W. direction (true) for about ten miles, when it reaches the centre of the fairway of the Strait of Juan de Fuca, which, by the chart, is in the latitude of 48° 17′ north and longitude 123° 14′ 40″ W.

Thence the line runs in a direction S. 73° W. (true) for twelve miles, to a point on a straight line drawn from the light-house on Race Island to Angelos Point, midway between the same.

Thence the line runs through the centre of the Strait of Juan de Fuca, *first*, in a direction N. 80° 30′ W., about 5¾ miles to a point equidistant on a straight line between Beechey Head, on Vancouver Island, and Tongue Point, on the shore of Washington Territory; *second*, in a direction N. 76° W., about 13½ miles to a point equidistant in a straight line between Sherringham Point, on Vancouver Island, and Pillar Point, on the shore of Washington Territory; *third*, in a direction N. 68° W., about 30¾ miles to the Pacific Ocean, at a point equidistant between Bonilla Point, on Vancouver Island, and Tatooch Island light-house on the American shore, the line between the points being nearly due north and south, (true.)

The courses and distances as given in the foregoing description are not assumed to be perfectly accurate, but are as nearly so as is supposed to be necessary to a practical definition of the line laid down on the chart and intended to be the boundary-line.

HAMILTON FISH.
EDWD. THORNTON.
JAMES C. PREVOST.

UNIVERSITY OF MICHIGAN
3 9015 01992 2288

www.ingramcontent.com/pod-product-compliance
Lightning Source LLC
LaVergne TN
LVHW020742120826
845150LV00010B/2357

* 9 7 8 1 4 1 8 1 9 4 4 1 3 *